11-22-78

Catch a Sunbeam

Illustrated by Kiyo Komoda

Florence Adams

Catch a Sunbeam

A Book of Solar Study and Experiments

Harcourt Brace Jovanovich   New York and London

Library of Congress Cataloging in Publication Data

Adams, Florence.
    Catch a sunbeam.

    Includes index.
    SUMMARY: Includes instructions for sixteen solar
experiments that reveal a variety of facts about the
sun and the uses of solar energy.
    1. Sun—Juvenile literature. 2. Solar energy—
Juvenile literature. [1. Sun. 2. Solar energy.
3. Experiments] I. Komoda, Kiyoaki. II. Title.
QB521.5.A3   523.7   78–52820
ISBN 0–15–215197–4

First edition
B C D E F G H I J K

Contents

Catch a Sunbeam

Worshiping the Sun

Have you ever thought about how it might have been to live in *ancient* times, thousands of years ago, without the benefit of even the most basic scientific knowledge? Imagine believing that the *sun* was a god who ruled the *earth;* a god who sailed on a ship across the sky each day, growing stronger on the way to the top and weaker on the descent to the opposite side. There the god would die of exhaustion in a blood-red sunset. At night the god would be put on a barge to ride beneath the earth until morning, and then be born anew to begin another fiery journey across the sky. You might also have believed that the earth was flat, that you lived in the center of it, and that the sky covered it like a dome. The ancients had every reason to think of the sun as a god. No one could control this hot, glowing ball, which sometimes brought them *heat* and *light,* but often hid from them, making the earth wet or cold.

All ancient people worshiped the sun in some way. The sun was the natural center of their religious concepts and of their various explanations of the events of nature. Religion today has nothing to do with *science* (which means the gathering of facts to explain the world around us), but the ancients' beliefs and their worship of the sun were also the beginnings of

An early depiction of the Egyptian sun god, *Ra*

the science of the sun as we now understand it. We know now that the earth and eight other *planets* travel around the sun, which is the center of the solar system; that the sun is a star; that the sky is open space filled with billions of other stars, many of which also have planets. We know too that the earth is a great ball with its surface covered with land and water and that no place on the outside of a ball can be the center.

How did people learn all the things we know today? It was not easy. It took a long time, beginning perhaps when some ancients became curious about things that occurred over and over—things like shadows moving, the temperature changing, or plants growing in warm times. A curious person here and there studied those happenings and made notes and charts—or rather, began to gather facts, *scientific facts.*

Today the sun has become the object of a new phase of scientific study. To replace earth's fast-disappearing *fossil fuels* (oil, gas, and coal) scientists are searching for other *energy* sources. Like the ancients, they are looking up, feeling the warmth of the mighty sun, and trying to develop ways to harness its power for use on the earth below.

To make your study of the sun, why not begin as an ancient scientist? Reach back in time by hundreds and thousands of years and observe the habits of this great heavenly body as an ancient might have done. Then, as you gather facts, you can use them to progress through the centuries to the present and even to make projections into the future.

Remember that scientists must keep notes, charts, and pictures of their studies and observations, so begin a new notebook for your *solar* experimentation.

You will need equipment for many of the *experiments*, and this is listed at the beginning of the experiment. However, during your solar exploration your curiosity and imagination may help you to develop different work materials to find the same scientific answers.

One final word. Sometimes you may have to start an experiment over because something interrupted—rain, for instance. Don't be discouraged. This happens to scientists all the time. But because a scientist is a person who never stops until an answer is found, you, too, must continue.

Discovering the Ancients' Theories about the Sun

Experiment 1: You Are an Ancient

It is 4,000 years ago. Go outdoors. Go out early in the morning when the sun is just rising. Notice where it comes from. A little later in the morning look again to see where the sun sits in the sky. (Just glance quickly at the sun; don't look directly at it because that can damage your eyes.)

Look again at noon. If you were an ancient you would know it was noon without a watch or clock. The sun has traveled from the place where it first appeared, up and over, until at noon it is at the highest point in the sky.

Look again in the middle of the afternoon. Finally, watch in the early evening as the sun sets and disappears below the horizon.

Where does it go? To the opposite side of the world from where it came, of course.

Make some notes or draw some pictures about what you observed: where the sun first rose, perhaps from behind a mountain or a building, and where the sun went down.

Tomorrow watch the whole process again.

What would you think about the sun and earth if you lived 4,000 years ago? If you lived on flat land with open space, you may have thought that the sky was a round cover like a dome. If you lived surrounded by tall mountains, it may have appeared that the mountains were holding up the sky. How could you, as an ancient, ever have guessed that the sky was really endless open space?

Think about your ancient world for a while. The sun is very powerful. It is easy to believe that it is a god or goddess ruling the earth.

Experiment 2: The Sun and Shadows

While you were standing outdoors observing the sun in the first experiment, did you notice how your *shadow* changed during the day? In this ancient experiment you will study your shadow more carefully to see what you can learn from it.

Equipment   Gather about a dozen hand-sized stones for markers.

You will also need a long measuring stick. You may use a yardstick, but you might want to make your own ancient ruler. Find a long, thin piece of wood or a straight branch about the length of a yardstick. Place four fingers side by side at one end of the stick, then scratch a mark on the stick to show the distance of the four fingers from the end. Next, move the fingers to the other side of the mark and scratch a second mark on the far side of the fingers. Keep doing this until you reach the other end of the stick. Your measuring stick will read "four fingers" instead of inches.

Finally, you will need a pole about 3 feet long. This could be another long stick or branch, but it must be very straight. This will be the shadow rod.

A few days before you begin the experiment, locate a large open space that is filled with sunlight all day long—a space at least 30 to 35 feet long. This is about ten times the length of the sticks. Also, listen to the weather forecasts. You will need sun all day, from sunrise to sunset.

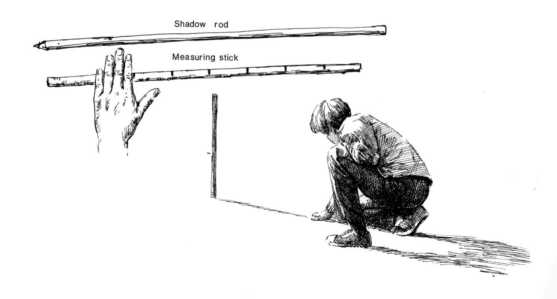

Shadow rod

Measuring stick

On the day of the experiment, get up very early, just as the sun is rising. Go to the open outdoor space you found, bringing your equipment, your solar notebook, and a pencil.

In the center of the space, stick the shadow rod deep into the ground so that it will not fall over. (It must stay there all day long.) Observe how long the shadow of the rod is.

Place one of the marker stones at the end of the shadow.

On a new page in your notebook write "Experiment 2." Also write down the time, perhaps 7 a.m. (We'll allow you, for this experiment, to use a watch or clock, although the ancients used *sundials* to tell time.) Now, using your yardstick or your measuring stick, measure the length of the shadow. If you use the measuring stick, count the number of scratches from the marker to where the rod is in the ground. If you use a yardstick, the measurement will be in inches. Write this measurement beside the time.

Come back in an hour and do the same thing, placing a new stone at the end of the shadow and measuring the new length of the shadow. Leave all the stones in place until the end of the experiment. Write the time and measurement in your notebook.

Do this every hour until the sun sets.

What do you notice about the stones on the ground? And what does your chart tell you about how the distances changed every hour? What have you, as an ancient scientist, proved? Think about your answer before reading on.

Sunlight cannot pass through the shadow rod, so it creates a shadow, or dark image. In the beginning of the day, the sun is very far off to the side of the rod and the shadow is very long. By the middle of the day, the sun is directly overhead and there is no shadow, or almost none. Then in the afternoon, the sun is on the opposite side of the rod, and the shadows grow longer again.

The stones on the ground go from one side of the stick to the other side. This means, to your ancient mind, that the sun moved from one side of the world to the opposite side, because that's what it appears to have done.

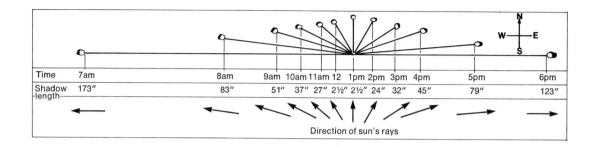

Time	7am		8am	9am	10am	11am	12	1pm	2pm	3pm	4pm		5pm		6pm
Shadow length	173″		83″	51″	37″	27″	2½″	2½″	24″	32″	45″		79″		123″

Direction of sun's rays

(As a modern you know that the earth moves around the sun, but remember, you are an ancient, 4,000 years ago, with no scientific facts gathered about the sun yet.)

When you look at your chart, you see that the distances got smaller every hour until noon, then got longer again.

Surely you have proved that something is moving! It does seem to be the sun, doesn't it?

(If your first experiment is made in Standard Time, the shortest distance may have been at noon. However, in the spring clocks may be set to Daylight Saving Time, to allow more daylight time for work or play. If so, in later experiments it may be that one c'clock will be the middle of your experiment, instead of twelve o'clock.)

Experiment 3: Winter, Summer, Where Is the Sun?

You may only read and think about this experiment, but if you were an ancient who sought to know more about the sun, you would really see it through. It would take, however, many years!

Remember what you did in Experiment 2 with the shadow? Suppose you could leave the marking stones and the shadow rod undisturbed for a long time. If you go out on the next sunny day you will see that the shadows fall in about the same places. And the next day it would be about the same.

16

This tells you that the sun repeats the trip around earth the same way every day. Or does it?

Try watching the pattern for a longer period of time—for a year. You can do this experiment every three months, on a sunny day in the middle of June, September, December, and March.

Equipment   This time you will need about 48 stones. You will also need paint: red, brown, blue, and green. Your measuring stick and shadow rod will also be needed.

Paint 12 of the stones red, for the summer (June) experiment. Paint 12 stones brown for the autumn (September) test, 12 stones blue for the winter (December) test, and 12 stones green for the test in spring (March). (Can you guess why these colors were chosen for the different seasons?)

Start in whichever month you choose, picking a day that will be sunny all day long. Repeat what you did in Experiment 2, placing marker stones at the end of the shadow of the rod every hour, measuring the distances, and making the chart in your notebook. Use the stones of the proper color for each season.

Leave the stones on the ground. Come back three months later, on a sunny day, and do the experiment again, using stones of the proper color for that season. Come back again three months after that, and again another three months later.

At the end of the four tests, you will see a curious picture in the stones. The red stones of June will almost be a straight line crossing the shadow rod. The blue stones of winter will form a curve farthest away from the shadow rod. The green and brown stones of spring and fall will lie between the red stones and the blue stones. Now, what can this mean?

First of all, it tells you that the sun does not travel the same path every day. From June to the beginning of autumn, the path of the sun overhead has changed and is farther away in September than it was in June. You will realize this if you notice that the noontime brown marker of September is

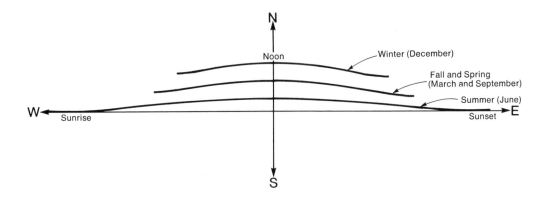

farther away from the shadow rod than the red noontime marker of June. The sun is directly over your head in June, but not in September. The blue noontime marker in the beginning of winter is even farther away than the brown noontime marker of September. The sun is even farther from the very center of the sky at that time. Also the weather is colder.

Finally, the green noontime marker of spring shows that the sun is coming closer to the center of the sky again. And the weather is getting warmer.

Does the pattern start all over again? Will the June markers fall in the same place as the year before? What course does the sun travel and how can you prove it?

For a scientist, proof comes from repeating an experiment over and over until the same thing has happened so many times that there is no longer any doubt that it will continue to happen in the same way. In this experiment an ancient might have had to do the same four tests for at least five years to reach the firm conclusion that the red summer markers will be the same every June, and the others will be the same in autumn, winter, and spring.

In five years, you, like the ancient, would have proved satisfactorily that the pattern of movement between the sun and earth repeats once a year. This discovery helped the ancients to make a *calendar*.

Five years is a long time to do an experiment, isn't it? Perhaps you understand now why it has taken so long to learn and gather scientific facts

through the ages.

Experiment 4: The Sun's Rays Bring Heat and Light

Did you notice, when you were doing the early experiments, that the day got brighter and brighter after the sun rose? Did you feel warmer around noon-time? Why?

Equipment   You will need an outdoor *thermometer* for Part 1 of this experiment, and a flashlight and a basketball for Part 2.

Part 1   Go again to an open space that will be in sunshine all day long. Go early in the morning and lay the thermometer on the ground. Wait a few minutes until the mercury in the thermometer has absolutely stopped moving and then read the temperature.

Go to the very same spot every hour and do the same thing. Make a chart of your readings, showing time and temperature.

What do you discover at the end of the day?

As the sun rises higher in the sky the *temperature* rises also, due to the directness of the sun's rays. (See illustration on page 20.)

After the sun rises, it brings light and also brings heat, though the intensity of some heat and light always gets diffused on the long trip from the sun by dust in the earth's *atmosphere* and other particles in *outer space.*

What determines how strong the rays of sunlight are is the direction from which they come to us. Do they come straight down, as they seem to do at noon on a summer's day, or are they skimming across the top of the earth, as they seem to do at sunrise? Let's do the second part of this experiment so that we may understand this better.

Part 2   Place a basketball at one end of a long, dark room. From about ten feet away, turn on the flashlight and shine it directly onto the ball. Where is the brightest circle of light? Where is it dullest? Draw a picture of what you see. Show the beam of light coming out of the flashlight to the brightest spot. Show the beam of light going to the dullest area. What is happening?

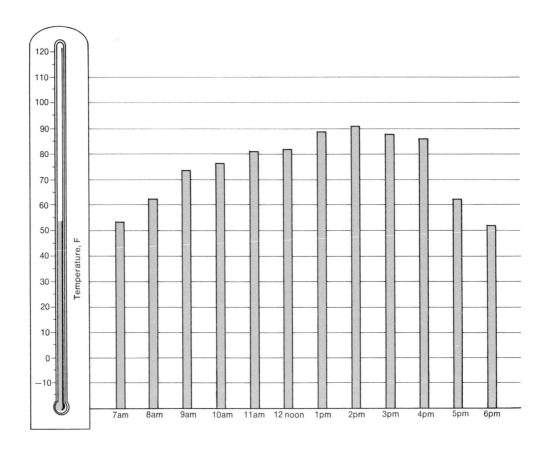

The beam of light from the flashlight that gives the brightest circle of light follows a *perpendicular* path to the ball, just like the line your body makes to the ground when you are standing perfectly upright. The light from the flashlight appears to give less light on the ball's outer edges since those areas receive the light at a smaller angle. The perpendicular path is the most direct route, then, and produces the strongest beam of light.

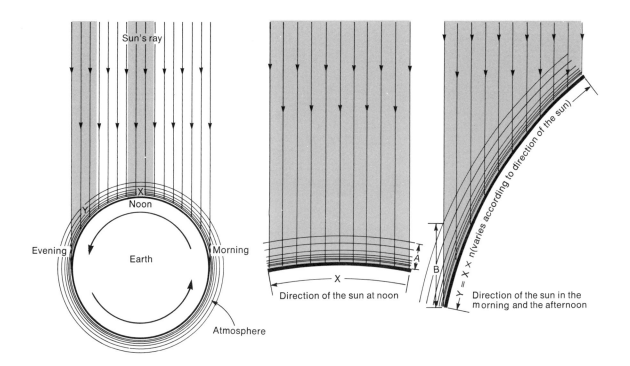

Sun's ray

Noon

Evening

Earth

Morning

Atmosphere

Direction of the sun at noon

$Y = X \times n$ (varies according to direction of the sun)

Direction of the sun in the morning and the afternoon

The sun seems cooler and dimmer in the morning and evening because the same amount of energy (shown by arrows) spreads over wider areas of the earth. Also, the sun's rays have to travel longer and on a diagonal path through the earth's atmosphere, losing a good portion of their heat and light. Compare the difference between "X" and "Y," also "A" and "B."

The flashlight is like the sun. Look at the illustration above of the sun and earth. At sunrise the straight, direct rays of sunlight and sunheat are passing across the top of the earth, not shining down. But at noon the path of the strong rays is directly down to the place we are, flooding the area around us with heat and light.

Discovering How the Earth Revolves Around the Sun

Throughout our experiments so far, we have talked about the sun's moving around the earth, which as ancients we would have believed to be true. But, as you know, the earth *revolves* around the sun.

We cannot do here all the scientific experiments to prove this, however, because keen observations, complicated equipment, and difficult mathematics are required for them. It was in fact less than 400 years ago that scientists were able to discover the truth about the movements of the sun, the earth, and the other planets in our *solar system,* because the *telescope* was not invented until the early 1600s.

Let us take a moment to think about some of the early scientists who studied the earth, the sun, and the solar system, and about their *theories.*

In Alexandria, in the second century A.D. there lived a Greek mathematician and *astronomer* named Claudius Ptolemy. He studied the heavens and spent his lifetime making careful observations and charts of what he saw. Finally, in A.D. 150 he published a report of his findings. Because he was a respected scientist, his theory was accepted.

In his report he stated that the earth was the center of the solar system, not moving from its spot, and that the five planets (the only ones then known) and the moon and the sun all revolved around the earth. It is not difficult to understand why his theories were believed, because observation could be made only with the naked eye and as you have also observed using only your eyes, the sun appears to be moving around the earth.

These theories were accepted for hundreds of years, although even among the ancients there were a few far-sighted thinkers who believed that the earth moved around the sun. Certainly other astronomers were doubtful about Ptolemy's ideas, especially when some of them were not supported by actual observations, but it was not until about 1543 that a different idea was suggested, the one we now know to be true.

Nicholas Copernicus was a Polish astronomer who doubted Ptolemy's theories. He too studied the heavens. His studies told him something different—that the sun was the center of the solar system and that the earth was itself a planet and, like the other planets, revolved around the sun.

It seems hard to believe now, but in the time of Copernicus the way the sun and earth moved was still a religious matter, and the church of the time would not accept the new theories of Copernicus. For one thing, if the earth was not the center of the *universe,* it meant that man might be a little less important in the scheme of things. Because the telescope had still not been invented, Copernicus could not readily prove his theories. Just before he died his papers were published, but only as curious ideas which most people thought were probably not correct.

But other astronomers who doubted Ptolemy's theory studied Copernicus's work. Nearly half a century after Copernicus's death an Italian astronomer named Galileo Galilei had developed a very fine telescope. Although the church's attitude had not changed, Galileo accepted the ideas of Copernicus and worked with his new telescope until he was convinced that Copernicus was right.

In 1632 he published his proof, but the church put him on trial, forced him to withdraw his ideas, and placed him under house arrest. Ten years later

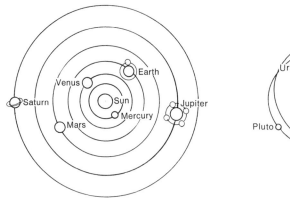

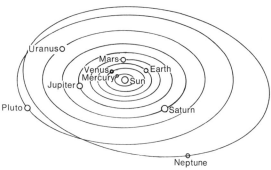

Solar system of Copernicus

Solar system of Kepler

Galileo died, a broken man, because much of the world did not believe him, any more than it had believed Copernicus, but other scientists continued his investigations with the telescope.

While Galileo had been working in Italy, another astronomer named Johannes Kepler had been working in Germany. Kepler and Galileo wrote to each other often about their findings. Kepler's work showed that the planets revolved in *orbits,* or paths, that were not exact circles, as Copernicus had suggested, but *ellipses,* which look like circles that have been squeezed a bit.

In England in the same year that Galileo died, 1642, another important astronomer and mathematician was born. His name was Isaac Newton. With his studies of the heavens he added some of the most important information which proved that Copernicus was right. One of the reasons he was able to do this was because he developed a far better telescope. It was one that used a curved mirror at the bottom of the telescopes to collect the light, instead of a see-through lens at the other end of the instrument. With this type of telescope he could see much clearer and farther out into space. Newton introduced the theory of *gravity* and was able with this to explain why the planets remained in orbital paths around the sun, instead of drifting away.

Ptolemy
(140 a.d.)

Nicholas Copernicus
(1473–1543)

Galileo Galilei
(1564–1642)

Johannes Kepler
(1571–1630)

Sir Isaac Newton
(1642–1727)

Gravity is a force acting between two bodies, by which each attracts the other. The forces of attraction between the sun and the earth work out so that earth revolves in a fixed orbit around the sun, and the same is true with the other planets.

Kepler had explained how the planets moved and Newton explained why. And the world believed at last.

As the telescope was improved, astronomers could study the heavens far beyond the solar system. They learned that the solar system, with the sun, its planets (now known to be nine) and other bodies, is part of a *galaxy,* or island of stars, called the *Milky Way.* In the Milky Way galaxy the sun is one of about 250 billion stars. The others are the stars we see at night. We cannot see all 250 billion of them ever, but on any clear night, with the un-aided eye, we can see about 2,000 of the stars in the Milky Way, and in the course of a whole year we could observe about 6,000, though not all at the same time, because we see different parts of the sky in different seasons. Consider 250 billion suns!

The Milky Way is not the only galaxy, however. There are about 100 billion other galaxies in the heavens. This entire vast space is called the universe, and out there are about 250 billion times 100 billion stars (250,000,000,000 $\times$ 100,000,000,000). Many have planets revolving around them. Perhaps there is even a planet just like earth out there. No one knows yet how many planets there might be, because they are as yet impossible to see. They are not powered by the same nuclear fusion that make stars shine. They shine only by reflected light.

(Have you ever wondered how far you can see with your naked eyes? Guess. Ten miles? A hundred miles? More, much more. You can see the sun, which is 93 million miles away. And you can see the stars in the Milky Way. The nearest star that we can see is 23.5 trillion miles away. And we can see others farther away than that.)

To get back to our experiments, you, no longer an ancient, have grown a few thousand years older, and much wiser. Now the world knows that the earth revolves around the sun. It has also learned that the earth *rotates* on a "tilted *axis*." What does that mean?

Experiment 5: The Earth's Tilted Axis

Equipment   Clay, a stick, a table, a protractor, some dry markers (red, dark green, light green, dark blue, and light blue), a piece of cardboard.

Form a round ball of clay, about the size that will fit inside your hands. Take the stick and push it up through the center of the clay ball.

Stand the stick straight up on a table and turn it around. The ball of clay turns too. Make a tiny scratch on the clay ball and turn the stick around once, until the scratch comes back to where it started. Our planet earth turns around once a day just like this—or almost.

Scientists have learned that our earth is somewhat like a huge *magnet,* where the *North Pole* of the "magnet" is at the top of the globe and the *South Pole* at the bottom. If you could draw a line from the North Pole to the South Pole, you would have something like the stick going through the ball of clay (though, to be precise, the geographic poles are some distance from the magnetic poles).

This imaginary line from pole to pole is called the axis around which the earth rotates. The clay ball rotates around the stick. The axis of the ball is the stick, which we can see, but the axis of the earth is not visible.

Now, tilt the stick a bit and turn it around. This is really how the earth turns around every day, the scientists tell us. In fact, they know that the angle of the tilt is about 23 degrees.

In the illustration there is a diagram of an angle of 23 degrees. Cut the same shape out of a piece of cardboard and draw a red line on the cardboard from the top right corner to the bottom left corner, just as shown. If you prefer, use a *protractor* to measure the angle. Also, draw a blue line on the cardboard.

Stand the cardboard angle marker up on the table on the blue edge of the cardboard. Stand the clay ball and stick in front of the cardboard, holding the stick tilted along the red line. Now, turn the stick and ball around in this tilted way. If you could stand on the sun and watch the earth turn every day and see the imaginary axis, this is how it would look—as tilted as the clay ball on the stick.

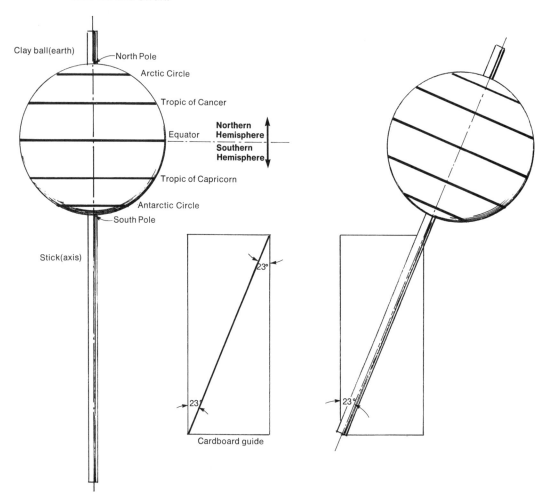

While the ball of clay is still soft, scratch some lines around it, as shown in the illustration, because it will be used in the next experiment. The lines circling around the globe are imaginary lines of *temperature zones.*

When the clay becomes hard, color the scratched circles with dry markers. Use red around the middle line for the equator. Above that, use light green for the Tropic of Cancer, and above that use light blue for the Arctic Circle. Under the equator use dark green for the Tropic of Capricorn; under that use dark blue for the Antarctic Circle.

Experiment 6: Winter, Summer, *Exactly* Where Is the Sun?

Winter is cold, summer is hot, spring and fall are warm-cool. You might guess that this is because the earth is closest to the sun in summer and farthest away in winter, but that is not the case. The earth is closest to the sun in spring and autumn and farthest away in summer and winter. Peculiar, isn't it, that when it's farthest away, the earth is either very cold or very warm. And when it's near, the temperature is not very hot or very cold. Why?

Perhaps you are guessing that this may have something to do with the earth's tilted axis. Now you must prove it.

Equipment The clay ball with the colored circles on the stick will be your earth. The cardboard angle marker will help you tilt the earth. (These were used in Experiment 5.) You will also need the table, a flashlight, and some books to prop the flashlight on. How many books? Holding the clay ball and stick tilted, guided by the angle marker, you must arrange the flashlight so that the very center of its light hits the very middle of the ball.

In the illustration there are four numbered positions on the table. You will move the clay ball earth from position 1 to position 2, then to position 3, then position 4. Place the books on the center of the table and position the

flashlight on the books. Each time you move the clay ball to a position, turn the flashlight to shine on the clay ball.

In order to do the experiment correctly, it is very important to move the clay ball the same way the earth moves. Therefore, you must always keep the front of the cardboard facing the same direction. In this experiment, it must always be facing side 4 of the table, with its two sides facing sides 1 and 3, and its back always facing side 2 of the table.

Start at position 1. Hold the tilted earth ball, with the stick resting on the table, close enough to the flashlight to see where the strongest beam of light hits the clay ball. Which temperature zone line gets the most light?

Move to position 2. See the diagram on page 32. Now which zone gets the most light? Move on to position 3, and finally to position 4, noticing in each place where the light is strongest.

Does the light from the flashlight (representing the sun) go to the same zone each time or to different ones? What does this mean? Before you read on, think about all you have learned from the preceding experiments and then try to figure out what this new experiment tells you.

In position 1, the strongest beam of light is on the Tropic of Cancer line. We live in this temperature zone. In the summer the strongest and most *direct rays of sunlight* and sunheat coming to the Tropic of Cancer bring the most heat (summer is the hottest season) and the most light (summer has the longest days).

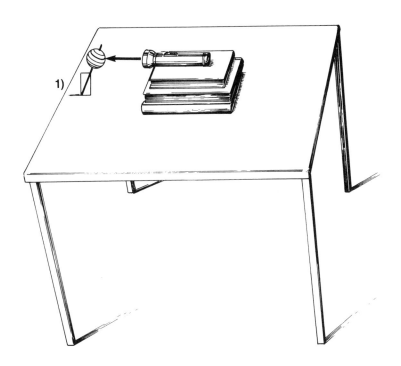

In position 2, the strongest beam of light goes to the equator. The Tropic of Cancer receives slanted rays from the sun, not strong direct rays. It is cooler when the earth is in this position as it revolves around the sun. Our season at this time is autumn.

In position 3, here in the Tropic of Cancer, our season is winter, because the straight and direct rays of sunlight are going to the Tropic of Capricorn, which is even farther away from us than the equator is. And for us it is even colder than in autumn. What season do the people who live in South America (in the Tropic of Capricorn) have at this time? Yes, it is summer.

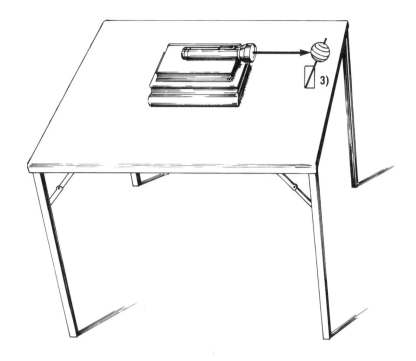

In position 4, finally it is spring in our zone, and the weather is getting warmer. There are buds appearing on bushes and trees. The very strong light and heat rays from the sun are coming closer to us again, for they are now at the equator.

And as the earth continues its yearly trip around the sun, it will soon be back to position 1, and we will have summer again. Summer is the only time that we receive direct rays. During the other seasons we receive only the less powerful *indirect* (slanted) *rays,* rays that have a longer trip through the atmosphere and lose some of their light and heat.

But would all this seasonal change happen if the earth's axis were not tilted? Try the experiment without tilting the stick. There is no change, is there? The strong light always goes to the same place. Therefore, it is because the earth's axis is tilted that we have different seasons.

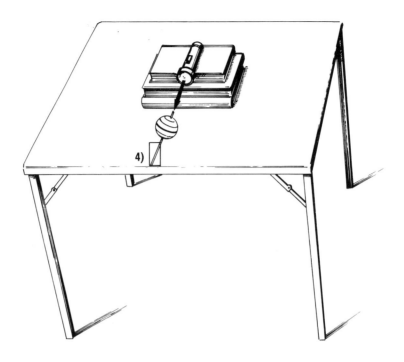

There is one more very important fact to learn from this experiment, which we will need to know for future experiments. What direction does the sunlight come from? The sun rises in the east and sets in the west, but what part of the sky does it occupy most of the time? The southern part or the northern part . . . or the center?

In the summer when the rays of the sun are direct the sun seems to travel across the center of the sky. During the other seasons we are receiving indirect sunlight coming up from the temperature zones beneath us, to the south of us, never from the northern regions. The sunlight comes from the south. It is the southern part of your house that receives the most sunlight all day long. And it is the warmest side. The northern side is the coolest and the shadiest.

Discovering How the Sun Can Work for Us

Sunlight can be put to work for us. "Energy" is a word that means the ability to do work. Sunlight is energy.

Experiment 7: Sun Energy Can Melt Ice

Equipment   2 ice cubes, each on a separate plate.

Place one plate with an ice cube outdoors in bright sunshine. Place the other ice cube and plate in a shaded spot outdoors.

Watch the sunshine ice cube. Watch the other. What happens?

The ice cube in sunshine begins to melt, much faster than the shaded ice cube does. Time how long it takes for the sunshine ice cube to melt into water. Time the melting of the shaded ice cube. The time periods are different. The sunshine ice cube melted faster because of the heat of the sun.

Leave the plate of water, the liquid melt of the ice cube, in the sunshine

35

for the rest of the day and watch what happens to it. The water begins to disappear. Where did it go?

Water can be solid, as ice, or liquid, as we drink it, or gas, a *vapor* that floats into the atmosphere. These are the three different states of matter: solid, liquid, and gas. The heat of sunlight melted water from its solid state ice, into its liquid state. Then the sun's heat *evaporated* the liquid into gas that drifted away into the air.

Experiment 8: Sun Energy Can Separate Salt Water into Fresh Water and Salt

Here you will see a remarkable use of *solar energy* doing very valuable work.

Equipment   A plastic food wrap bag about 10 by 14 inches in size; two disposable aluminum platters, one about 6 by 8 inches, and the other at least 8 by 10 inches; tape; flat black paint (you must always use flat dull paint, not shiny enamel. The enamel will reflect away some of the sun's rays; flat paint will not); a piece of wire about 50 inches long; a jar of salt water from the sea or from a salt lake or salt pond.

Paint the inside of the small pan with the flat black paint and let it dry. Cut two sides of the plastic bag open so that you have a flat piece of plastic 20 by 14 inches.

36

You are going to make a *solar still,* a device to manufacture salt. It looks somewhat like a tent. Using the wire, construct the framework of a tent. The framework should be bigger than the small pan and just fit inside the large pan.

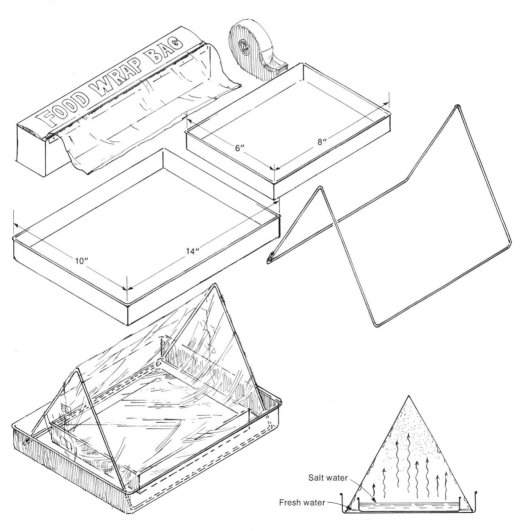

Salt water

Fresh water

Sit the frame in the large pan. Wrap the plastic around the frame and the large pan. The pan is the inside floor of the tent. Leave one side flap open, like a camping tent, and seal the rest all around with the tape.

Fill the small pan half full of salt water and carefully slip the pan into the tent without spilling any water. (If you do spill some, remove the small pan, wipe away the spilled water, and begin again.)

Seal the side flap lightly, so that you can open it later without too much disturbance.

Let your solar still sit in the sunshine all day, or maybe for a few days, and watch what happens.

In a very short time, droplets of water appear on the inside of the plastic cover and slowly roll down into the large pan. After a while, slip your finger through the flap end and dip it into the water collecting in the large pan. Taste your finger. Is it salty? No. The water collecting is fresh water, without salt in it. Why?

Water and salt are two different materials that, mixed together, make salt water. The sun in heating the salt water causes some of the water part of the salt water to get hot enough to evaporate into vapor which floats up onto the plastic. There the vapor collects as liquid drops and slides down the sides of the tent to the big pan. As this happens the level of the salty water is going down, because the water part is leaving.

Soon there will be no water left, only salt. If there had been no plastic tent, the evaporated water would have drifted off into the atmosphere, just as it did in the ice-cube experiment.

You can't drink salt water. For one thing, it just makes you more thirsty. Wouldn't a gadget like this be handy to have if you were stranded on a ship in the sea without any fresh water to drink?

In many places near salt water, salt is made in much the way you have done it in this experiment. In other places, where large salt deposits were left by the ice ages of long ago and buried underground by the eroding land that piled on top of it, salt is mined.

Experiment 9: Sun Energy Can Burn Paper

Equipment A *magnifying glass* and paper of different types: typing paper, tissue paper, white toilet paper, and newspaper.

Do this experiment about noontime when you know that the sun's rays are the hottest.

Lay the samples of paper on the ground outdoors in the sunlight. Use the thickest white blank paper first.

Hold the magnifying glass close to the paper at such an angle that the sun's rays pass through the glass onto the paper as the tiniest possible circle of light.

BE CAREFUL OF FIRE!!

A magnifying glass is a curious object. Here in our experiment it is actually changing the direction of the sun's rays, squeezing them closer together. The little dot of light on the paper has many, many more rays hitting it than it would without the magnifying glass. This means that there is more heat coming to that spot.

You will see that nothing happens very fast until you try the newspaper. Then a hole burns through right away! Why?

This is a tricky question. The reason is that the paper was both black and white.

Try the newspaper again near a picture. Hold the glass so that the dot of light is half on the black edge of the picture and half on the white part of the paper. The black part burns first.

What color shirt do you wear in summer? A white shirt lets you feel cooler than a dark blue, doesn't it? Even yellow is cooler. The reason for this is that each color reacts differently to the sun's rays. White bounces the rays away, *reflects* them, while black *absorbs* the heat of the rays, capturing it. Other colors reflect some light and absorb some, depending on whether they are dark or light, as we see in the next experiment.

Probably you have seen a rainbow. Or have you ever let sunlight pass through a *prism* (a triangular-shaped piece of glass)? Then you have noticed that white sunlight is really an arrangement of colors. This arrangement is called the *spectrum.* (See the illustration on page 41.)

The colors of the spectrum are, in order, red, orange, yellow, green, blue, and violet, but they seem to merge together because of mixtures of colors that are side by side, such as blue-green between blue and green.

Sunlight is really "white," although it seems to be *invisible,* or *transparent,* yet when it passes through a prism—or through raindrops, as in the case of a rainbow—the white light breaks up into a spectrum of all the colors that make it up.

White is a reflection of all colors. Black is an absorption of all colors. Another way of saying this is that white is all colors; black is no color.

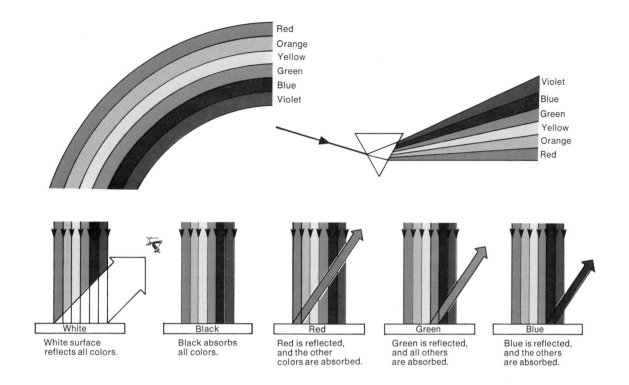

Red
Orange
Yellow
Green
Blue
Violet

Violet
Blue
Green
Yellow
Orange
Red

White	Black	Red	Green	Blue
White surface reflects all colors.	Black absorbs all colors.	Red is reflected, and the other colors are absorbed.	Green is reflected, and all others are absorbed.	Blue is reflected, and the others are absorbed.

Experiment 10: Color and the Sun's Rays

Equipment   Blank white typing paper, dry markers (black, dark blue, red, and yellow), and the magnifying glass.

On the typing paper, color a one-inch square of each of the four colors. For a white square, draw an outline with a pencil.

Take the paper and magnifying glass outside into the sunshine at noon-time. Again use the glass to squeeze the sun's rays together—to *concentrate* them on a small spot. However, in this experiment you want to find out how long it takes each color to burn, so get a slightly bigger spot this time. (Also, be careful not to burn yourself or your clothing.)

41

Start at the black square. Right away a tiny hole begins to burn through the typing paper.

Next do the blue square. Almost as fast, but not quite. Next the red. It takes a bit longer than the blue square. The yellow takes longer still. And finally the white square. (Are you still waiting for that one?)

What fact have you learned?

The darker the color, the more heat it absorbs, heat that can cause a fire if there is enough of it. The lighter the color, the less it absorbs and the more it reflects away.

Black absorbs the most heat, white the least.

Experiment 11: Sun, Water, Black, and White

In Experiment 7, we saw that the sun's heat can change solid ice to liquid water and then to gas. In Experiment 8 it separated salt water into fresh water and salt.

For the remainder of the experiments we will test this power for specific purposes. How can we make water hotter? Hot enough to wash our dishes, hot enough for a bath, hot enough to heat our home? How can we do this with solar energy?

Equipment   Two disposable aluminum cake pans; flat black paint and flat white paint; outdoor thermometer.

Paint the entire inside of one pan black; paint the inside of the other white. Let the paint dry completely before starting the experiment.

You will need three or four midday hours of full sunlight. Fill each pan with cold water and place the pans outside in the sun. Take the starting temperature of the cold water and mark it down in your notebook beside the starting time of the experiment. (A good time to do this is between 10 a.m. and 2 p.m.)

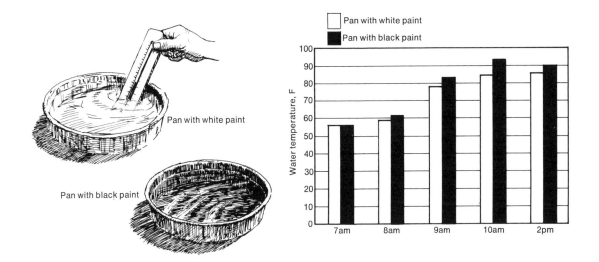

Pan with white paint

Pan with black paint

Pan with white paint

Pan with black paint

Water temperature, F

Take the temperature of the water in each pan every hour and note it beside the time in your book.

(A note about the thermometer: When you are not using it, keep it out of the sun in a glass of cold water, which will be about 65 degrees. After you take the temperature in the white pan, put the thermometer in the cold water again, then use it in the black pan. Do this in all the thermometer experiments: keep the thermometer out of the sun and let it start at a cold reading. One other important thing: a typical outdoor thermometer only goes as high as 120 degrees. Whenever the mercury appears to be rising near that limit, remove the thermometer, for it could break and leak mercury which is a very dangerous and poisonous substance. If this should happen, record such a reading as "over 120 degrees" and do not let the loose mercury get on your skin or clothes.)

What does your hourly chart of the reading tell you?

The water in the black pan gets hotter than the water in the white pan. Did you guess this might happen after the color experiment? Yes, black absorbs heat while white reflects it (sends it back). The heat collected by the black metal is transferred to the water. Of course, the water in the white pan also gets somewhat hotter, just as any water normally does sitting in the sunshine.

Let's try making the water in the black pan even hotter, hot enough to wash dishes with.

Experiment 12: Sun, Water, Black, and Glass

Equipment

Two disposable aluminum cake pans, both painted with flat black paint (you could paint the white pan of Experiment 11 black, since it won't be used again); a pane of glass big enough to cover one pan completely; and again the outdoor thermometer.

Just as in Experiment 11, fill both pans with cold water, taking the starting temperature and writing it in a new chart in your notes. Then, cover one of the pans with the pane of glass.

Take the temperature of the water in each pan every hour from about 10 a.m. until 2 p.m. Be careful when taking the temperature in the glass-covered pan. Do not cut yourself on the glass, and keep your eye on the mercury as it rises, for again you may discover it wants to go too high.

Glass

What happens this time?

The water in the glass-covered pan got *very* hot (perhaps 116 degrees) *very* fast. It's certainly hot enough for a bath, isn't it?

If the uncovered black pan got hotter than the white pan in Experiment 11, and then the glass-covered black pan got hotter than the uncovered pan, the reason must be the glass. Why?

The answer is that some of the heat in the water of the uncovered pan escaped back into the atmosphere. On the other hand, some of the heat in the water of the glass-covered pan was kept from escaping by the glass.

Glass is one form of *insulation.* Insulation is material that prevents the passage of heat. In winter windows keep the heat in. Heat cannot pass through certain other materials, such as wood, asbestos, and wool, which are also good insulators. This is why you wear wool clothes in winter, to keep your body heat from escaping into the colder surroundings.

There are materials that do allow heat to pass through, materials that hold it and pass it on to other substances. Water, as you have seen, is such a material. Another is metal. These materials are called *conductors,* because they carry (conduct) and transfer heat.

With all of this information, we can finally do our most difficult and most important experiment. It is one that scientists have been doing for a number of years, and they will continue doing as they try to improve their skills by what they learn with each new experiment.

Experiment 13: Constructing a Solar Furnace

There are a number of ways that buildings are heated. Some houses are heated by steam, which is made when water is boiled in a *furnace,* the steam then travels through pipes and radiators, carrying heat to all the rooms.

Other houses are heated by hot water, which is also heated in a furnace, but not heated as hot as steam. Pipes carry the hot water through the house to radiators, which, as the name suggests, *radiate* heat. The pipes and radi-

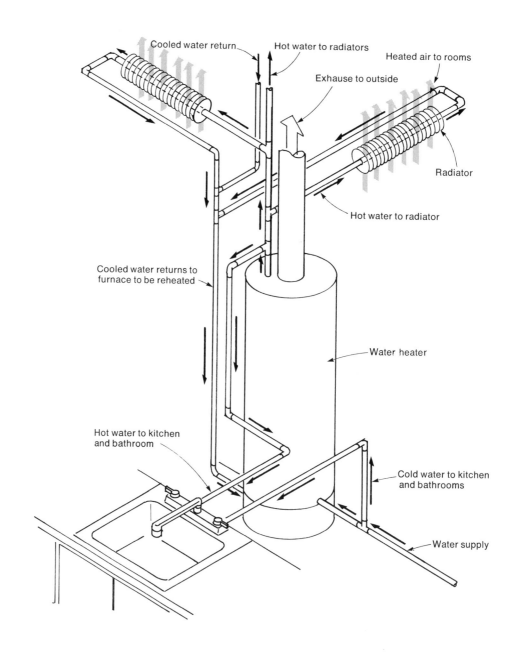

Cooled water return

Hot water to radiators

Heated air to rooms

Exhause to outside

Radiator

Hot water to radiator

Cooled water returns to
furnace to be reheated

Water heater

Hot water to kitchen
and bathroom

Cold water to kitchen
and bathrooms

Water supply

ators are made of metal (conductors) and allow the heat to pass through from the water to the rooms.

There is also hot-air heat. Air is heated by being blown through a furnace and then is forced through tunnels, or ducts, leading to screened openings in all the rooms.

Houses can be heated by electricity. Electric heating works somewhat like a toaster—electricity comes through wires that get red-hot and heat the house.

These are the common forms of heating.

A furnace is an apparatus that burns some kind of *fuel* to create enough heat to cause water or air to get much hotter. The substances that are used are coal, oil, or gas. These are the fuels for the furnace fires. (Electricity may also be used to heat water and air, but this can be an expensive method.)

Coal, oil, and gas are called fossil fuels because they are the remains of plants and animals buried millions of years ago while the earth was still forming. Buried under tons of debris from the early earth, the plants and animals decayed and changed their chemical composition, eventually becoming materials that burn well.

A serious fuel problem now exists, which the world is finally beginning to acknowledge—we are running out of fossil fuels. In the United States, some scientists have calculated that only about a 50-year supply of oil and gas is left. For the whole world, at the present rate of burning, there may only be enough to last until the year 2100.

What can we substitute for fossil fuels? What fuel will not run out? What substance will not *pollute* our earth as burning fossil fuels has done?

Diagram shows a typical oil or gas hot-water heater for heating a house. Hot water from the heater is piped to radiators in rooms; then the radiators transfer the heat from the water to the air in the rooms.

Some people have suggested using *nuclear energy,* the power that results from changing atoms. In fact, there are about sixty plants in our country already producing electricity by nuclear energy. Some experts tell us that there is only a small chance of accident, since safeguards are used to prevent the dangerous leakage of *radioactivity* that causes cancer. But they do admit there is a chance of accident. That is why many people want to limit our reliance on nuclear power until we can be even more certain about its safety.

Is there a substitute? Consider that the sun is expected to keep shining for 6 billion years more.

Shall we try to build a solar furnace or *solar collector?* The fuel will be the sun. We will collect heat from the sun's rays on a piece of black-painted metal, transfer this heat to water, and store the heated water in an insulated container to keep it hot.

Equipment   Thermometer; 8-ounce baby-food jar; heavy transparent plastic tape; flat black paint; red dry marker; cup with spout; funnel; a piece of glass 7 by 8 inches (or a thick, hard piece of plastic of the same size); two pieces of wood 3/4-inch thick, one 12 by 16 inches, one 8 by 8 inches; disposable aluminum pan with accordion-fold bottom (7 by 9 1/2 inches); disposable aluminum pan with flat bottom (6 by 8 inches, or bigger); saw; hammer; some 1/2-inch and 2-inch nails.

Preparation   (1) Accordion-bottom pan. Cut off both of the short sides. Cut V grooves in one corner of each of the long sides at (a) and (b) as shown in the diagram on page 50. Paint the entire inside surface flat black and let dry completely.

(2) Large piece of wood (12 by 16 inches). Cut out section (c) as shown. The section measures 5 by 2 1/2 inches and is cut 2 inches away from the 16-inch side. Across the top of the cut, draw a line (X), from one 16-inch side to the other, and slant the line very slightly up toward the right side.

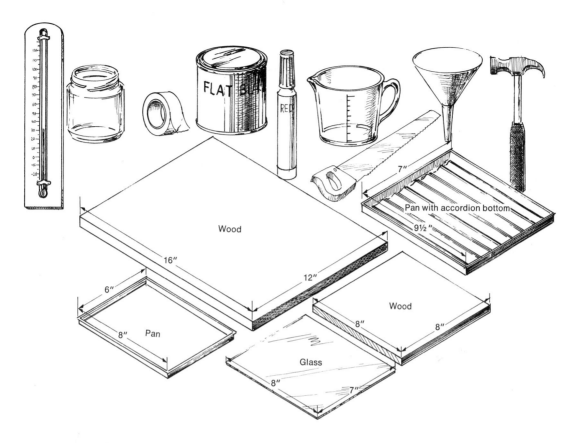

(3) Small piece of wood (8 by 8 inches). Number the corner points 1, 2, 3, and 4, as shown in the diagram. Draw a diagonal line across one corner to the other as shown in diagram (3) and cut the wood in half along this diagonal line (e).

These angled pieces of wood will be used as braces to tilt the collector to an angle of 45 degrees. (Measure the angles of the corners of the wood, if you like, with your protractor. They are all 45 degrees.) A solar collector should be tilted to receive the most sunlight, somewhat the way you tilted the magnifying glass in Experiment 9, and should vary according to the *latitude* you live in, but a good average all-year angle for our temperature zone is 45 degrees.

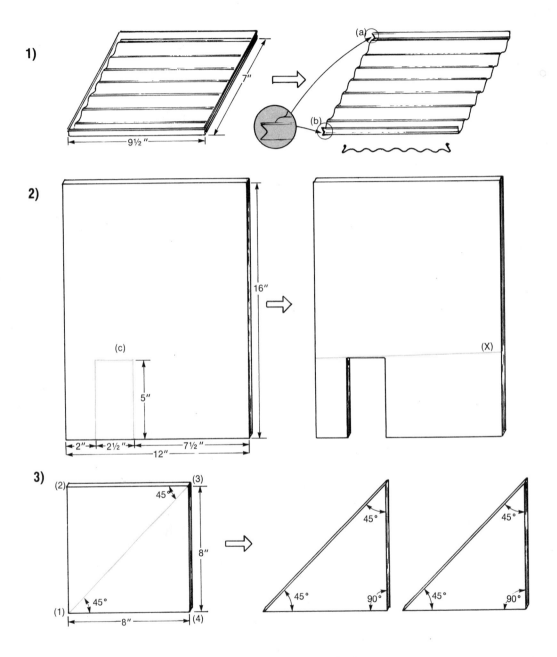

4)

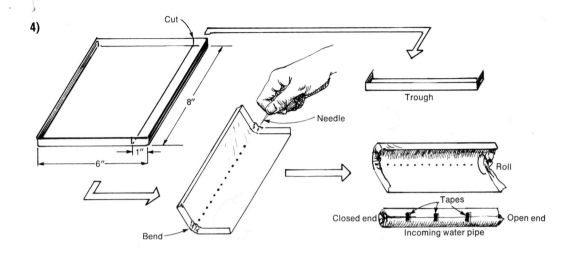

Cut

8"

1"

6"

Bend

Needle

Trough

Roll

Tapes

Closed end   Open end

Incoming water pipe

(4) Flat-bottomed disposable pan. This will provide two pieces of the collector, the "pipe" for incoming water at the top and a trough to collect the heated water at the bottom.

Cut a piece off about 1 inch from the 8-inch side to make the trough.

Bend the other piece in half, the long way, and along this bend, in the center 6 1/2 inches, make holes about 1/2 inch apart with a thick sewing needle. Now roll the piece into a circle, leaving the bend there, for it must fit into the V grooves of the black pan. Close one end of the "pipe" bending the edges in, and tape it. No water should leak out this end. Leave the other end open, but bend one edge up a bit. This is the end to pour water into.

Assembly

(1) Nail the angle braces onto the back of the large piece of wood, on the back corners, as shown in the diagram. See page 52.

(2) Hammer two nails (a) and (b) into the line (X) on the front of the large piece of wood, one 5 inches from the left side, the other 4 inches from the right side. Set the trough on this line on the nails. Nail the trough to the wood, hammering the nails into the upper corners (c) and (d).

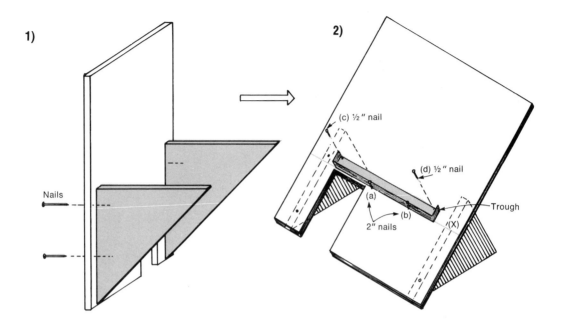

1)

Nails

2)

(c) ½" nail

(d) ½" nail

(a)

(b)

2" nails

(X)

Trough

(3) Put the black pan down into the trough and lay it flat on the wood. Hammer two nails (e) and (f) into the upper corners of the black pan to hold it in place, then two nails (g) and (h) outside, near the trough, to keep the black pan from moving to left or right. Bend the front face of the trough closer to the black pan, curling the edges of the trough a bit to tighten it.

(4) Very carefully holding everything, puncture a bunch of holes, making a big hole, at the bottom of the trough, directly over the center of the cut-out section, which is where the jar to catch the water will be put.

(5) Sit the rolled "pipe" pan into the V grooves of the black pan. Outside, at the top, in the center, hammer in a long nail (i) and then hammer it down a bit around the "pipe" to keep it in place. Next hammer a nail (j) at the left end outside, and also another nail (k) on the right end, to keep the "pipe" from moving from side to side. The nail on the right could be hammered right through the open end of the "pipe."

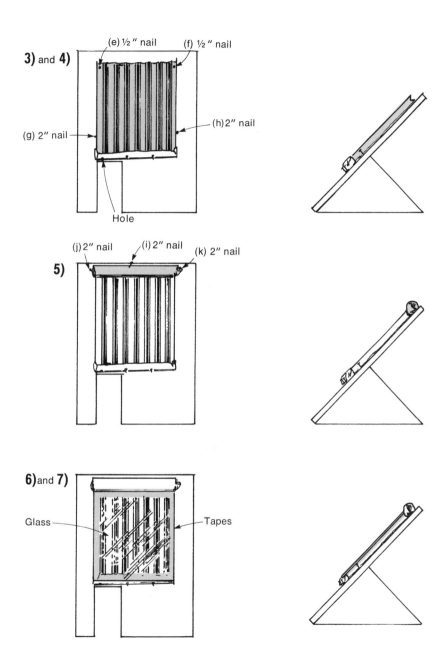

3) and 4)

(e) ½″ nail
(f) ½″ nail
(g) 2″ nail
(h) 2″ nail
Hole

5)

(j) 2″ nail
(i) 2″ nail
(k) 2″ nail

6) and 7)

Glass
Tapes

(6) Lay the glass into the trough and then flat on top of the sides of the black pan.

(7) Tape the glass all around to seal the collector. Tape the top of the glass to the "pipe," tape from near the bottom of the glass over around the top edge of the trough, and tape the side edges of the glass to the sides of the black pan.

What you have constructed vaguely resembles what is called a "flat-plate collector." It is a solar furnace that will use solar heat as its fuel to heat water. Will it work? Try it.

On a very sunny day, take the collector outdoors at about 10 a.m. and let it sit, tilted, facing south, until about noon, letting the black metal get hot.

At noon, begin the test. Place the baby-food jar, filled with water that is the same temperature as the outdoors, into the opening at the bottom of the wood, under the hole in the trough. Take the temperature of the starting water and write it down. It may be about 65 degrees.

(In very cold winter weather you will have to do this experiment indoors, in front of a window facing south, where the sun is streaming in. At 10 a.m., when you set the collector in front of the window, also set the jar of water in some shady place in the room, so that when you start the experiment at noon, the water will be at room temperature. The reason for this winter approach is that our little furnace will be too drafty to allow the water to heat outdoors. The results should be about the same.)

Step 1 Pour the water from the jar into the pouring cup; put the jar back in place.

Step 2 Using the funnel, pour the water from the cup very slowly into the opening in the pipe pan. It will drop through the needle holes, drip down along the black pan, collect in the trough, and flow through the hole into the jar.

Step 3 Quickly take the temperature of the water in the jar (you will see that it has been raised a few degrees).

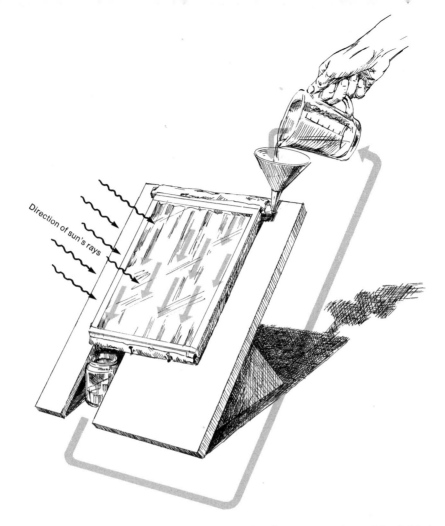

Direction of sun's rays

Step 4   Repeat steps 1 and 2 five times and then take the temperature. Much higher. (At this point in my last experiment, the water had been raised from cold at 65 degrees to 74 degrees.)

Step 5   Repeat steps 1, 2, and 3 five more times. The temperature will become higher. (In only ten pours, the water temperature can be raised 15 degrees, and as you continue, the temperature will keep rising.)

Even though our solar furnace is very crude, what can you learn from this experiment?

The sun heated the black-painted collector pan because metal is a conducting material and black absorbs heat. Glass is a good insulator and kept the heat inside. This heat was transferred to the water droplets as they passed down along the collector. If this heated water were kept in an insulated container it would stay hot for quite a while. How about using a *Thermos*?

In this experiment, your moving hands have been like a pump, transferring the water from the jar to the cup and pouring it into the pipe. Now let's imagine a faster, better system. A Thermos replaces the jar. A tube comes from the bottom of the trough into the top of the Thermos, one end of the tube sealed to the trough, the other end sealed into the lid of the Thermos. From the bottom of the Thermos a tube comes out to a pump, continues up to the "pipe," and is sealed into the "pipe," the pump, and the trough. A pump is like a fan that moves the water by pushing it. Here it would draw the water from the Thermos and push it up the tube into the "pipe."

Some insulation stuffed behind the black collector would help keep heat from escaping out the back, making your collector far more efficient.

This is the way a commercial solar collector works. Collector panels are placed on the roof facing south. Pipes connect them to an insulated water storage tank in the basement. A pump is attached along the pipe to move the water up to the roof when the collector is hot enough to reheat the water.

Simplified diagram of water heating by solar energy. Water or chemical fluid treated with anti-freeze solution (1) is pumped to solar collector (2). Solar-heated fluid (3) is then drawn to the heat exchanger (4) attached inside the conventional water heater with an oil, gas, or electric heating system (5). Here the heat from the fluid is transferred to water and piped to uses around the house (6). When solar energy is not available, the conventional heating system will take over. (A heat exchanger is a device that efficiently transfers heat from one thing to another without directly mixing the two.)

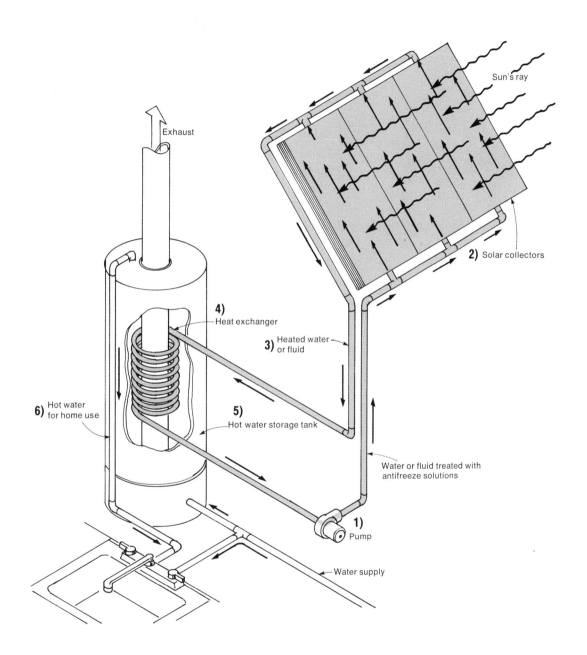

Exhaust

Sun's ray

2) Solar collectors

4) Heat exchanger

3) Heated water or fluid

6) Hot water for home use

5) Hot water storage tank

Water or fluid treated with antifreeze solutions

1) Pump

Water supply

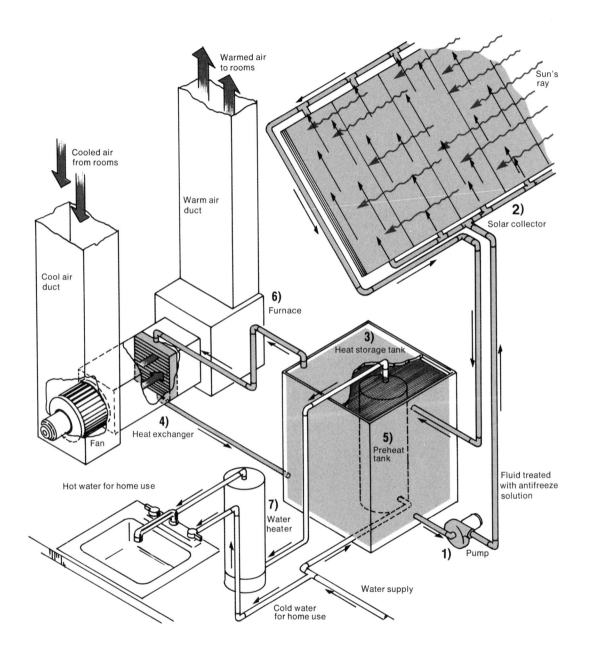

Warmed air to rooms

Cooled air from rooms

Sun's ray

Warm air duct

Cool air duct

2) Solar collector

6) Furnace

3) Heat storage tank

4) Heat exchanger

5) Preheat tank

Fan

Hot water for home use

Fluid treated with antifreeze solution

7) Water heater

1) Pump

Cold water for home use

Water supply

The heated water flows back down from the collector panels to the storage tank. The hot water in the tank can be drawn off for washing as well as for heating.

There are many different ways to design solar heating systems, but this is the general idea. A great many collector panels are needed to provide enough heat for an entire house, but only a few to provide hot water.

Now you are truly a sun-scientist in the future. In our country there are currently only a relatively few buildings using solar energy. But every day more people are beginning to consider this method of heating, because of the energy crisis and because of their high fuel bills. And the very best thing about using a solar furnace is that the fuel is free!

Solar energy for water and room heating. **The fluid (1) is heated by the solar panel (2) and stored in a large insulated heat storage tank (3). As needed, the fluid is drawn to the heat exchanger (4) to heat rooms and at the same time heat water in the preheat tank (5). When solar energy is not fully available, the conventional furnace (6) and water heater (7) will raise the temperature of the air and water to the desired level.**

Camping Out with the Sun

On a camping trip not every day can be a sun day, but there are ways to utilize the help of the sun on the days it does shine forth.

Experiment 14: Using the Sun to Find Direction

Perhaps you have a watch but not a *compass* . . . and you are lost.

First remember the ancients' shadow experiment (Experiment 2). The sun rises in the east and travels across the southern part of the sky until it sets in the west, as in Experiment 1.

Then, as we saw in that experiment, the stones fall in a half circle (flattened) from east to west, in the southern side of the flattened circle. And if we drew a line from the shadow rod to the noon rock it would point due south (Experiment 2).

Here is the way to use your watch to tell where south is when it isn't noon.

Point the hour hand of the watch toward the sun. South will be halfway between the hour hand and twelve o'clock. (Go forward to twelve o'clock in the morning; go backward to twelve o'clock in the afternoon.)

If you want to be absolutely sure you are pointing the hour hand exactly toward the sun, lay the watch on the ground and stick a match in the ground beside it. Move the watch around until the shadow of the match falls across the hour hand in a line to the time opposite.

Experiment 15: Using the Sun to Tell Time

Perhaps you have a compass but no watch. Here is a simple and workable sundial that you can make out of paper and carry with you.

Cut it exactly the same size as the diagram and draw the same lines, indi-

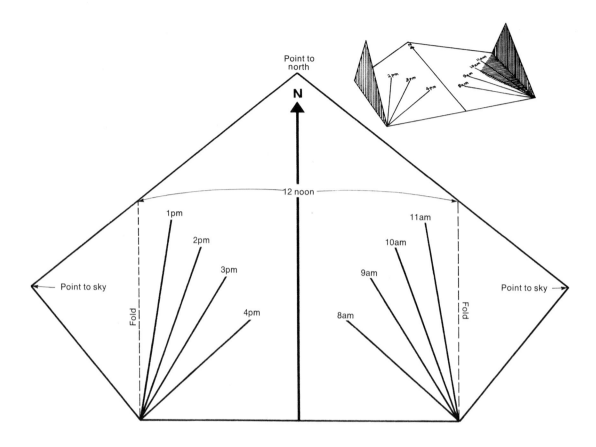

cating the numbers. Fold the side pieces up so they will point to the sky when you lay the sundial on the ground. Point the sundial north. The folded sides will cast a shadow on the paper and tell you what time it is. (Use the compass to determine where north is . . . or remember that it is where the shadows point at noon, because then the sun is due south.)

Experiment 16: Using the Sun to Cook Your Food

Making a solar grill is a project that will give you something more than a toy. You will be able to "barbecue" with sunlight instead of charcoal and fire. The grill is portable so you can take it camping or to the beach and not have to worry about finding fuel. It will cost nothing in energy to grill frankfurters, shishkabob, or fish.

In order to cook by the sun it is necessary to concentrate the sun's rays. You did this when you concentrated the sunlight with a magnifying glass. In this project you will use a different method of concentrating the sun's rays —a *parabola*. A parabola is a curious curve. Imagine a curved mirror held under the sun. When the sunlight is bounced off the mirror all the rays go to the very same place. This spot is called the focal point. Because this happens, the sun's rays are concentrated at this point, which gets more sunheat as a result. See below.

Equipment   2 sheets of graph paper, 10 squares to the inch; 2 3/4-inch-long nails; 16 1 1/4-inch No. 6 screws; 3/4-inch-thick pine wood, 4 pieces 18 inches by 5 1/2 inches and 2 pieces 14 by 5 1/2 inches, cut from an 8-foot length of 1 by 6 inches; 2 2-inch-long pieces of wood about the width of a ruler; *Mylar,* 1 sheet 14 by 20 1/2 inches and 2 sheets 18 by 4 1/2 inches; skewer 15 to 16 inches long, or a 16-inch length of stainless steel welding rod, 1/8-inch in diameter.

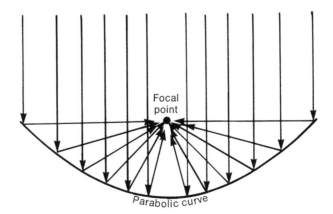

Focal
point

Parabolic curve

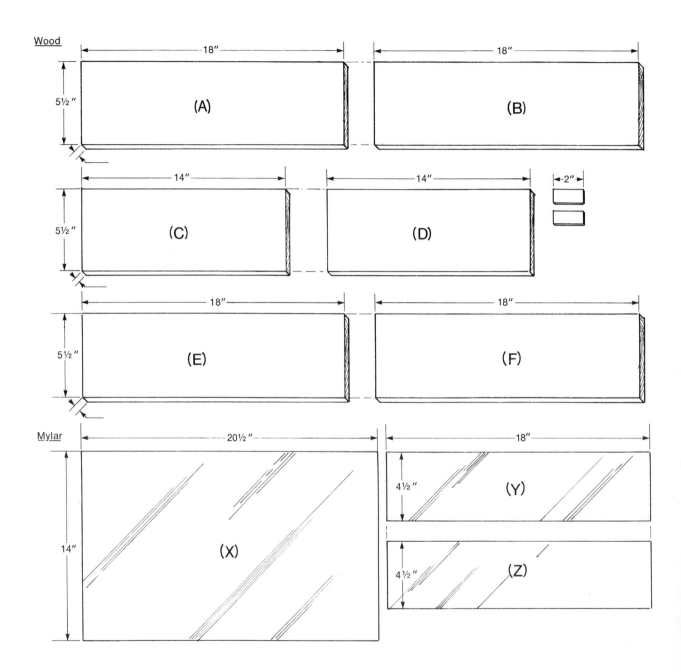

The primary piece of a solar grill is a piece of Mylar (a very shiny silver plastic) curved as a parabola. A box is constructed to hold the Mylar, and a skewer, placed on top of the box across the deepest curve of the parabola, becomes the focal point.

Preparation   (1) To begin with, construct a parabola on the graph paper. Tape both sheets together in the back. Draw a line across the top and begin numbering from the left across the top, at every inch mark: 9,8,7,6,5,4,3,2,1,0,1,2,3,4,5, 6,7,8,9. Along the left margin indicate the inches down from the top line by writing the numbers 0,1,2,3,4,5, etc., at the inch marks. Next, place an "x" under each, the number of inches down listed in the table:

	inches		inches
0	4.5	5	3.1
1	4.4 (under each 1)	6	2.5
2	4.3	7	1.75
3	4.0	8	0.9
4	3.6	9	0

Connect the xs to form a curve. This is the parabola. Cut along the top line and around the curve. This is the pattern you use to cut the wood and the Mylar.

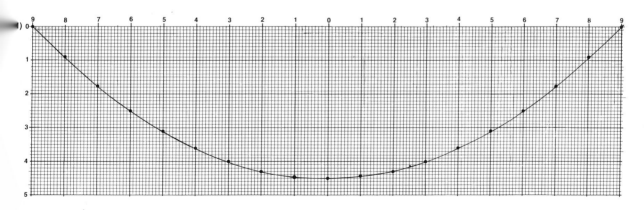

(2) Lay the pattern on piece A of the wood and trace the line of the curve onto the wood, as shown below.

Do the same on piece B.

Also use the pattern to trace a curve onto Mylar pieces Y and Z.

2)

With scissors, cut out the curved parts of the Mylar from pieces Y and Z.

Next, saw piece A of the wood along the pencil line, dividing it into pieces A_1 and A_2. Do the same with piece B to obtain pieces B_1 and B_2.

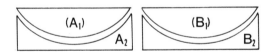

(3) Predrill holes and screw the four sides together (A_2, C, B_2, D).

3)

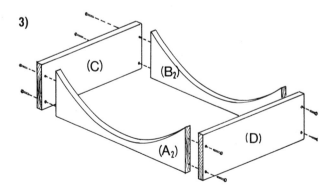

Lay the large sheet of Mylar (X) along the curves of sides A_2 and B_2. Although it really isn't necessary, you may want to glue the Mylar to the wood.

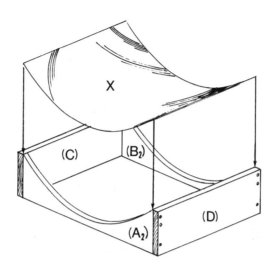

Next, glue Mylar Y to wood A_1 and Z to B_1. After they have dried, predrill two holes and screw piece A_1 to piece E as shown on the diagram. Do the same with pieces B_1 and F.

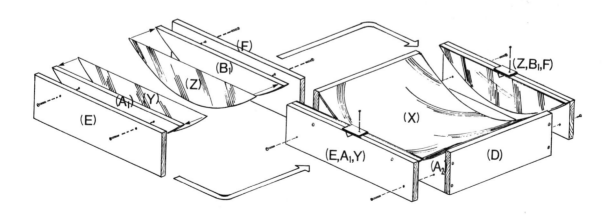

Saw a small V in the center of each, as shown below. The skewer will sit in these grooves.

Nail the skewer holder, the 2-inch thin wood piece across the V. Nail on one side only, so the holder can be slid away in order to remove the skewer. Also nail a holder on piece B_1/F.

Finally, sit the section A_1/E on top of the curved side A_2. Predrill two holes and screw A_1/E onto A_2. Sit section B_1/F on the curved side B_2. Predrill two holes and screw B_1/F onto B_2.

If you are unable to find a skewer of the proper length, you may use an 18-inch length of stainless steel welding rod, 1/8 inch in diameter.

In order to line up the grill with the sunlight, first place it lengthwise facing the sun. Then tilt it up until you see the brightest reflection from the underside of the skewer onto the Mylar. You can find this by watching the center of the Mylar and noticing how the intensity of light from the skewer changes as the grill is raised and lowered.

Once you have the proper angle, wedge the grill in a tilted-up position by using bricks or thin pieces of wood.

You will soon discover that you can cook many things with your portable solar grill.

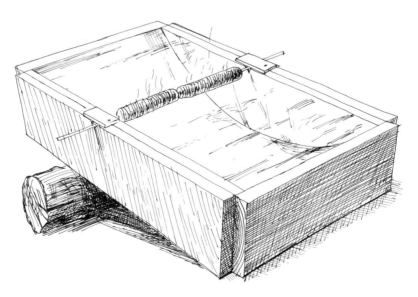

Catching Sunbeams

In the future solar energy may become a common type of fuel for heating buildings and houses and producing hot water. Scientists have also developed a system for using the sun's energy to produce cool air for homes and offices. Solar-powered batteries may someday be used to power automobiles and perform other mechanical operations.

However, solar technology is still in the experimental stage, and equipment is too expensive for widespread use.

Before long scientists, we hope, will develop cheaper methods of capturing and using the sun's energy to make it more readily available to all of us. When that happens, the earth will indeed be reaching toward the sun and catching many sunbeams.

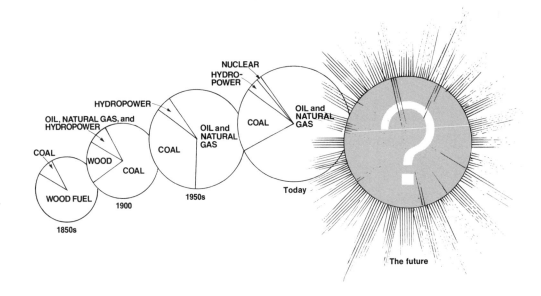

Glossary

Absorb. Cause to disappear or lose identity.

Ancient. Belonging to times past, particularly the period from 2000 b.c. to the fall of the Roman Empire in the west, a.d. 476; also a person living in those times.

Astronomer. A scientist who studies the universe outside the earth's atmosphere.

Atmosphere. The gases that surround heavenly bodies.

Atom. The smallest particle of a substance that cannot be separated by chemical means.

Axis, earth's. The imaginary line, through the center of the earth from the North Pole to the South Pole, about which the earth rotates.

Calendar. A system by which the year is arranged by days, weeks, and months.

Compass. A magnetic device that determines direction by pointing north; also, an instrument used to draw circles.

Concentrate. To bring together to one point, thus increasing strength.

Conductor. A material that carries and transfers heat.

Direct rays of sunlight. Rays that reach a point on earth after traveling on a straight path from the sun and are therefore strong. (See *Indirect rays of the sun.*)

Earth. The planet on which we live, which is the fifth largest in the solar system and the third in order from the sun; its distance from the sun is approximately 93 million miles.

Ellipse. An oval shape.

Energy. The capacity to do work; types of energy include chemical, electrical, heat, mechanical, and nuclear. (See *Nuclear energy.*)

Evaporate. To change from a liquid to a gas.

Experiment. A test or procedure to check a supposition or theory.

Fossil fuels. Chemically altered remains of plants and animals buried deep in the earth millions of years ago and preserved, the source of such fuels as oil, gas, and coal.

Fuel. A substance that can provide heat or power.

Furnace. A device in which heat is produced. The conventional furnace includes a chamber for burning fossil fuels; a solar furnace is a collector. (See *Solar collector.*)

Galaxy. A large collection of stars bound together by gravity. There are about 100 billion galaxies in the universe. (See *Milky Way.*)

Gravity. The force of attraction between all bodies, people, things, and earth; between earth and other planets and the sun; between stars and other stars in a galaxy; between galaxies and other galaxies in the universe.

Heat. Energy from the motion of *molecules.* Heat energy can be converted to other types of energy. The sun is our most important source of heat and is responsible for plant life today, as well as for the fossil fuels we now use for heat.

Indirect rays of the sun. Rays that reach a point on earth having traveled on a slanted path, thus losing some intensity. (See *Direct rays of sunlight.*)

Insulation. Material used to prevent the passage of heat. A good insulating material is one that has many air holes. A *vacuum* is the best insulation.

Invisible. Incapable of being seen because the substance does not contain enough molecules; the air around us is an example.

Latitude. Angular distance north and south of the equator.

Light. Particles of light energy traveling in waves from the body emitting the light energy into the space the waves travel.

Longitude. Angular distance east or west measured from the meridian at Greenwich, England.

Magnet. A piece of iron having the property of attracting iron and also of pointing north and south when suspended. (See *Compass.*)

Magnifying glass. A double convex lens, which increases the apparent size of the object viewed. It also can be used to concentrate the sun's rays.

Matter. Any substance that has weight and occupies space. Matter can exist in solid, liquid, and gaseous states.

Milky Way. The galaxy to which our solar system belongs. It consists of about 250 billion stars.

Molecule. The smallest physical unit of a substance, composed of atoms joined in a group. The grouping can be defined by the type and number of atoms joined. For example, water, H_2O, is composed of molecules made up of two hydrogen atoms plus one oxygen atom.

Mylar. A type of shiny plastic.

North Pole. Northern point of the earth's axis, latitude 90 degrees North, and *longitude* 0 degrees East/West.

Nuclear energy. Energy produced by altering the nucleus of an atom. One form results from a nucleus splitting into two parts (nuclear fission), and another form from nuclear fusion, by which a heavier nucleus is formed from two lighter ones.

Orbit. The path a planet or satellite travels as it revolves around another body.

Outer space. Space beyond the atmosphere of the earth.

Parabola. A shape made by the intersection of a cone with a plane parallel to its side.

Perpendicular. At right angles to a given line or surface.

Planet. Body revolving around the sun or another star. The major planets of the solar system, in order from the sun, are Mercury, Venus, Earth, Mars, Jupiter, Saturn, Uranus, Neptune, and Pluto.

Pollute. To make unclean.

Prism. A three-sided glass that causes sunlight passing through to disperse into the color spectrum.

Protractor. Instrument for measuring angles, shaped as a half-circle.

Radiate. To emit rays of light and heat.

Radioactivity. A property of some elements which spontaneously disintegrate into smaller elements, giving off radiation as this happens.

Reflect. To cast back heat, light, sound.

Revolve. To move in a curved path around a center.

Rotate. To move around a center or axis.

Science. Knowledge organized to discover general truths or the operation of general laws, especially relating to the physical world.

Scientific facts. Results from scientific research and correlation.

Shadow. The dark figure or image projected by some body that has blocked the passage of light; the absence of light.

Solar. Pertaining to the sun.

Solar collector. A device that collects sunheat on its metallic surface and then transfers the heat to the medium passing across the metal, usually water or air.

Solar energy. The power that comes from the sun as light and heat.

Solar still. A device that uses the sun to separate salt water into fresh water and salt.

Solar system. The sun, together with the planets and other bodies that revolve around it and are held in orbit by gravity.

South Pole. Southern point of the earth's axis, latitude 90 degrees south, longitude 0 degrees east/west.

Spectrum. The band of colors produced when sunlight is dispersed into rays of different wave lengths: red, orange, yellow, green, blue, and violet, and all manner of color hues between.

Sun. The star that is the center of our solar system. Constant nuclear fusion on the sun brings us heat and light energy.

Sundial. Instrument that tells the time of day by a shadow cast in sunlight.

Telescope. An instrument used to make distant objects appear larger and nearer. (A celestial telescope is one in which the image is gathered at the far end of the telescope and is magnified by the smaller end, the eyepiece.)

Temperature. A measurement of the degree or intensity of heat or cold.

Temperature zones. Areas on the earth where the typical temperature is commonly very cold, mild, or very hot. Starting at the northern part of the earth, the temperature zones are the Arctic Circle, Tropic of Cancer, Equator, Tropic of Capricorn, and Antarctic Circle.

Thermometer. An instrument to measure temperature.

Thermos. A container for preserving the temperature of beverages and other food. A vacuum is the common insulation in a Thermos.

Thermostat. A device that regulates the amount of heat produced by a heating system according to a predetermined temperature.

Theory. A more or less scientific idea or supposition that explains some subject, based on a collection of test results that illustrate the premise.

Transparent. Allowing the transmission of light without altering the rays. For example, objects can be seen through glass without distortion.

Universe. All existing things, galaxies, solar systems, suns, planets, satellites, and all inhabitants.

Vacuum. A space containing little or no air or gas.

Vapor. The gaseous form of a substance normally solid or liquid.

Index